Volume Six

PAINTING

Volume Six

PAINTING

Curtis J. Badger

STACKPOLE BOOKS

Published by
STACKPOLE BOOKS
Cameron and Kelker Streets
P.O. Box 1831
Harrisburg, PA 17105

Printed in Hong Kong

10 9 8 7 6 5 4 3 2 1

First edition

*Cover design by Tracy Patterson with
Caroline Miller*

Interior design by Marcia Lee Dobbs

Cover photo: English sparrow carved and painted by
Floyd Scholz. Photographed by Roger Schroeder,
reprinted with permission from *Wildfowl Carving
and Collecting* magazine.

Library of Congress Cataloging-in-Publication Data

Badger, Curtis J.
    Bird carving basics.

    Contents: Vol. 1. Eyes — [etc.] — v. 5. Texturing
v. 6. Painting.
    1. Wood-carving. 2. Birds in art. I. Title.
TT199.7.B33   1990   731.4'62   90–9491
ISBN 0–8117–2334–8 (v. 1)

Contents

Acknowledgments

Painting carved birds is an intense, time-consuming process that requires full concentration. That's why I appreciate having had the opportunity to look over the shoulders of the three artists represented in this book as they went about the painting process.

Larry was painting a pintail for World Level competition in the 1990 Ward World Championship when I visited, and he generously let me spend a day in his shop taking pictures and asking dumb questions while he tried to concentrate on vermiculating the sidepockets of his pintail drake. It turned out to be a beautiful bird, and it was a privilege to spend some time watching Larry go about the creative process.

Rich put up with me not only for two painting sessions, but also for a session on stoning and burning his scaup drake, which appeared in Volume 5 of this series, *Bird Carving Basics: Texturing.* It was interesting to be able to see Rich texture the bird, and then to come back a few weeks later to watch him paint the head and bill of the drake. Painting the head of a scaup drake would seem like a fairly straightforward process—after all, it appears to be basically black, with a little dark blue thrown in. But such is not the case, as we will see in the following pages.

I hadn't intended to include the brant in this book, but while I was at Rich's shop I noticed a pair of beautiful unpainted brant gunning decoys on a shelf. Rich said he was planning to paint them, so I invited myself to his shop for a third time.

Bob Swain is an old friend who never seems to complain when I show up with camera and lights. I've looked over his shoulder on a number of projects, but on this one I did so at a discreet distance. Bob uses a combination of paint and fire to produce traditional birds, and I didn't need to have my eyebrows singed.

These three talented artists were very generous in sharing their time with me and in passing along some of their painting techniques to you. I appreciate their artistry, and their patience.

Introduction

In bird carving, painting is the last step in a complicated series of processes. First, there is the planning and engineering, then the carving, the addition of detail and texture, and finally painting. Painting completes the process, but is dependent on all that has gone before.

When an artist paints a scene on canvas, the act of applying paint is a singular act. It begins and ends right there on the canvas. But in bird carving, you are dealing with a three-dimensional object that already has its well-planned contours, its highlights and shadows, its textures. For a successful carving, your plans for painting the bird should not begin after the bird has been carved, but as part of the carving process itself.

Rich Smoker was thinking about painting when he designed the scaup drake in Chapter 3 with a tuft of feathers on the back of its head. Larry Tawes, Jr., was thinking about painting when he carved feather splits in the pintail he paints in Chapter 1. When painting on canvas, you use pigment alone to create highlights and shadows. But when painting a carved bird, the pigment must complement and extend visual devices already present.

Details added during the texturing process are amplified during painting. A shallow dimple or a split in the edge of a feather can be emphasized in painting by applying a thin wash of black or burnt umber to the area. The pigment settles into the textured area, darkens it, and increases definition. When carving and texturing, the artist previsualizes the painted bird, planning the location of shadows, highlights, and other visual elements.

Although a carved bird is three-dimensional—and thus creates its own shadows and highlights—it often is necessary to emphasize them. As Rich Smoker paints the head of the scaup drake, for example, he adds subtle highlights during the painting process. The head of the bird is dark blue-black, but to paint it straight blue-black would rob it of all depth and realism. By beginning with an almost psychedelic palette of colors, Rich emphasizes the form and contour of the head by creating highlights that underlie the blue-black color of the head.

One of the advantages of acrylic paint is that it is a thin, transparent medium. It not only allows the finely textured detail to show through, but because it is transparent, the painter can apply light undercoats beneath dark colors to emphasize highlights, as Rich does on the head of the scaup.

This book covers a variety of painting techniques ranging from blending paint to vermiculation of decorative birds, painting gunning decoys, and distressing paint with fire. These sequences are designed to provide a starting point for you as you develop your own style of carving and painting. If you enjoy making highly detailed, decorative birds, then you will want to pay particular attention to Rich Smoker's blending technique and Larry Tawes's methods of painting and vermiculating a pintail sidepocket. But if your goal is to make simple carvings in the traditional gunning style, you won't want to miss Rich's session on painting a brant or Bob Swain's demonstration on burning paint.

Painting is an inexact science. It's impossible to tell you, when painting the head of a scaup for instance, to use precisely this amount of mars black, this amount of permanent green, and this amount of purple to arrive at the correct color. Good painters seem to go by feel rather than formula. They use the bird as a palette.

They also emphasize the need for good reference material, such as live birds, study skins, photographs, and videotapes. Larry and Rich both have aviaries, and both use study skins for color reference. You might not have a backyard aviary, but your local zoo might have a good collection of waterfowl, and many good books are available that contain sharp color photos.

Other than reference material, all you'll need are some brushes, paints, and a carved bird to work with. Your selection of brushes should reflect your style of painting. For decorative painting with acrylics, you'll need good quality brushes in a variety of sizes. Small brushes are necessary for fine detail such as vermiculation, and large brushes are needed to apply washes of color over a wide area. Start with a half dozen or so in different sizes, and let your specific needs determine future additions to your collection.

Both Larry and Rich work with acrylic paints, and Bob Swain uses oil-base colors, which are necessary for the burning process. Larry and Rich like acrylics because they are thinned with water, can be applied easily in thin washes, dry in a reasonably brief time, and produce good tonal values. Some experimentation with both oils and acrylics might be called for before you settle on a single medium.

One term that will keep popping up *déjà vu*-like throughout this book is "thin wash." In painting a three-dimensional, textured object such as a carved bird, you want to build color values slowly by applying numerous thin coats of paint. This lends depth and dimension to the color, and it allows meticulously wrought textured detail to show through.

For example, when Rich paints the head of the scaup drake, he begins with a surprising palette of bright colors. These are blended on the bird itself, and later are darkened by applications of thin washes of raw sienna and black. The bright colors eventually become very subdued, but their presence gives the head its lifelike depth of color and iridescence.

Bob Swain uses a variation of the same theme in painting his dowitcher. A wash of color is applied, burned off, and then the process is repeated until he arrives at the patina he wants. Sometimes two applications will do the job, sometimes it takes four or five. With some practice, you'll get a feel for the color combinations and the effect of burning.

I should emphasize that the painting procedures shown here are considered starting points. Try the techniques and determine which are relevant and helpful in your own work. The idea is not to imitate what someone else is doing, but to borrow a few techniques and then apply them to your own particular style and vision. That's what art is all about.

1
Larry Tawes, Jr.
Vermiculating a Pintail

Larry Tawes, Jr., a thirty-two-year-old carver from Salisbury, Maryland, got interested in wildfowl art in 1970. His father, after spending some time with the noted carvers Steve and Lem Ward of Crisfield, Maryland, began carving birds, and Larry junior became interested through his father. "It was a typical father-son thing, I guess," Larry says. "He got interested in carving, and what he did, I wanted to do."

Larry's grandfather is a Crisfield native and the tradition of waterfowl hunting and decoys was a part of Larry's life growing up. When Larry was older, he worked with his dad for eight years as a waterman on the Chesapeake Bay and for several more years in the masonry business. Both of the Taweses began carving as a hobby, and they slowly started to sell birds as public interest in carving increased. In the late 1970s Larry, Sr., decided to devote full time to bird carving, and shortly thereafter Larry, Jr., did also.

Larry, like his dad, started by making gunning birds. But in the mid-1970s, when interest in decorative birds began to grow, he began searching for ways to make detailed, highly realistic carvings. As a result, he developed tools and techniques that fit his tastes and goals in carving.

Today Larry works in a comfortable studio just outside Salisbury. His shop is bordered on two sides by a large aviary, and a glass wall on one side provides a constant view of pintails, wood ducks, blacks, wigeons, teals, tree ducks, and assorted other waterfowl. Larry is a talented carver and painter of realistic birds, and his aviary gives him the opportunity to study every nuance of appearance and behavior.

The pintail Larry is painting in this session was an entry in the 1990 Ward World Championship. The drake pictured here represents half of a pintail pair Larry carved and painted, then mounted on an intricate piece of driftwood. A photo of the completed carving is included at the end of this section.

Larry begins painting the sidepocket feathers of the pintail by applying a base coat to the bird. The bird has been carefully textured with a high-speed grinder and a burning tool, and Larry has primed it for painting with two coats of Deft lacquer diluted 20 percent with thinner.

Larry uses Jo Sonya, Liquitex, Aquatex, and Permalba acrylic paints. "Most carvers like to settle on one brand of paint, but I use four different types. After twenty years' experience I've had a lot of time to play with different types of color," says Larry. "In the beginning it's important to apply the coats in very thin washes. As the color builds up, I thicken the paint somewhat. The key to using acrylics is to allow the color to build up over the areas you've textured. You don't paint a bird with a single coat of paint."

Larry begins painting at the rear of the bird, applying a wash of titanium white to the belly and a mix of Jo Sonya raw umber and black to the rump, primary, and tertial feathers. A small amount of raw umber is added to the white paint to give it a slightly creamy value. The paint is diluted with water so only a thin coat of color is applied at a time. "The first coat is applied in a thin wash and is drawn into the wood, into the burned details," says Larry. "I'll darken it later with heavier washes."

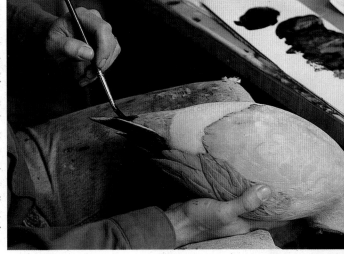

As the black and raw umber is applied to the rump, it is drawn into the texture of the wood, as seen here.

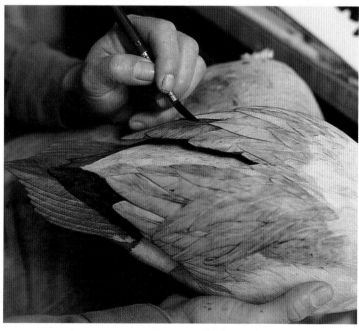

Now Larry applies a wash of black and raw umber to the primaries and tertials. "I'm basically emphasizing the detail of the burning process," he says. "I want the burned areas to show through when I put the grays on the tertial feathers."

Larry applies two more washes, and the wing tips begin to darken.

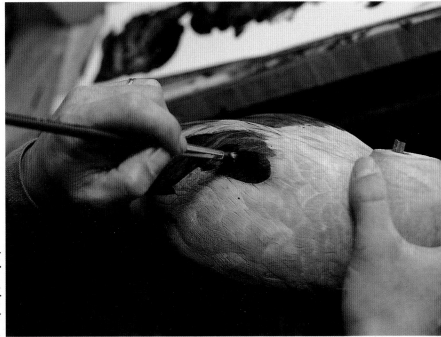

He repeats the process on the other side of the bird, applying washes of Jo Sonya raw umber and black.

Now Larry mixes the color for the sidepockets: 10 percent Jo Sonya black, 40 percent Jo Sonya warm white, 40 percent titanium white, and 10 percent Liquitex raw umber. Larry mixes the colors on a clean sheet of white paper.

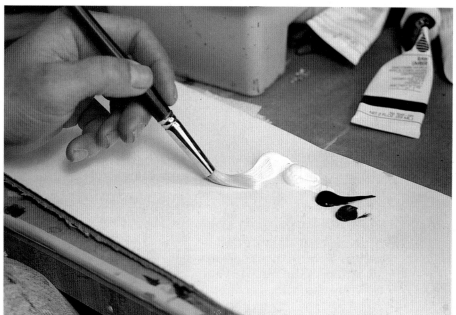

The mixture yields a smoky gray color, which Larry applies with a number 10 white sable brush to the sidepockets. He will apply three washes of the same color to the sidepockets, allowing each coat to dry before applying another. Sometimes he uses a small hair dryer to dry the paint between coats. The advantage of acrylics is that they dry very quickly, usually in fifteen minutes or less under normal conditions of heat and humidity.

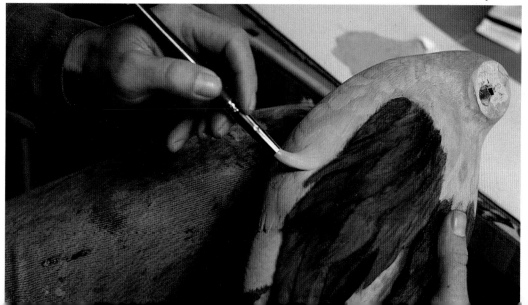

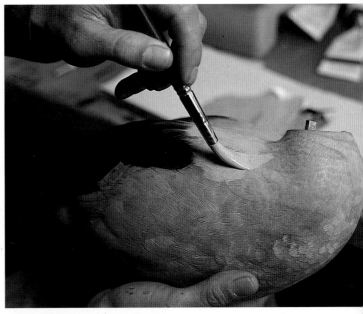

"Sometimes when you're painting a large area such as the sidepockets, you'll get small bubbles in the paint," Larry says. "You need to get rid of them before they dry. I go over the area with a large dry brush and pull the bubbles out. If they harden, they'll ruin the paint job."

The same color is applied to the back of the pintail, and to the other side.

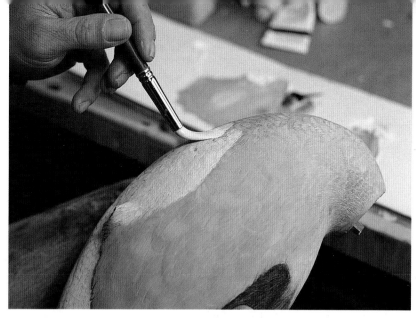

The breast of the pintail gets a preliminary wash of titanium white mixed with warm white and a touch of raw umber.

As you're painting, be careful when handling the bird not to get moisture or oils from your skin on previously painted surfaces. Larry washes and dries his hands periodically during the painting process. Sometimes he wraps the bird with cloths or paper. He is reluctant to wear cotton gloves because he is afraid of dropping the bird.

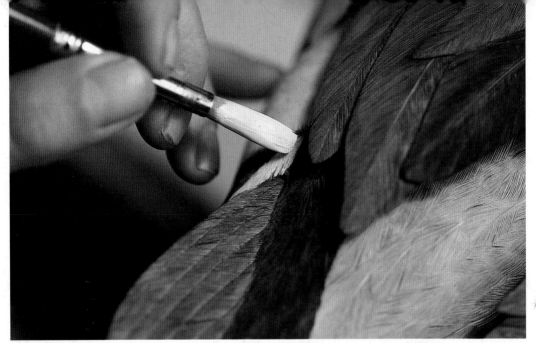

Larry applies a wash of the same white used on the breast to the area of the back where the wings cross.

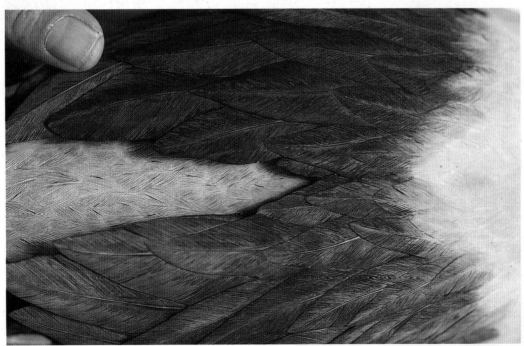

This close-up shows the folded wings and the smoky gray wash blended into them.

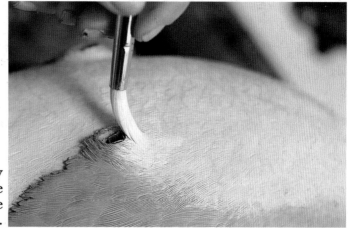

Along the breast, Larry blends the white into the smoky gray color of the sidepockets.

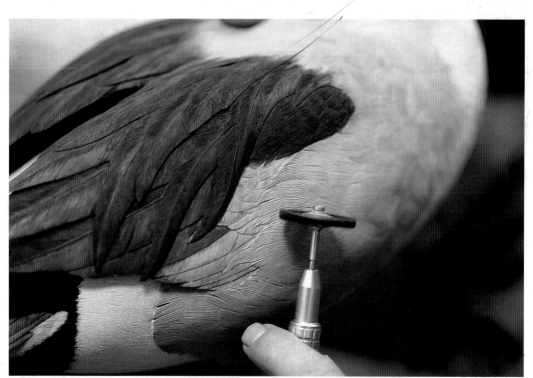

Before he begins the next step in painting the side-pockets, Larry uses a small buffing wheel on his high-speed grinder to clean the area. "Buffing cleans any debris out of the textured areas and smooths the surface, which will make your vermiculation much sharper," he says.

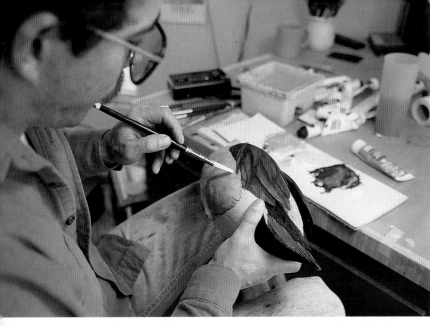

Now Larry begins dry-brushing a very light mixture of titanium white and raw umber across the flow of the feathers. This is done with the brush nearly dry, so only a small amount of paint adheres to the surface of the bird.

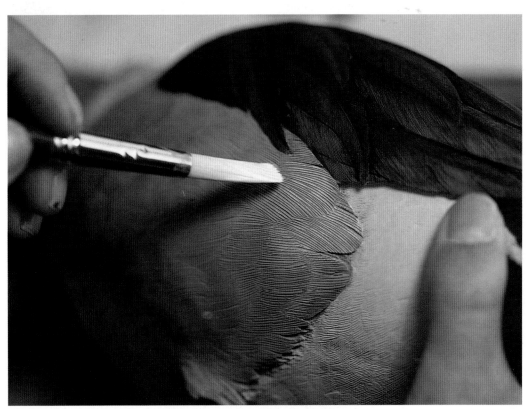

This technique adds highlights to the sidepockets and provides a light background for the vermiculation, which will be added next.

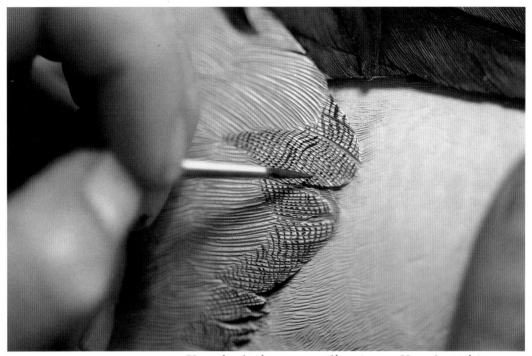

Vermiculation, according to my New American Heritage Dictionary, is defined as "motion resembling that of a worm." Essentially, Larry is creating hundreds of little worm tracks across the sidepocket feathers of the pintail.

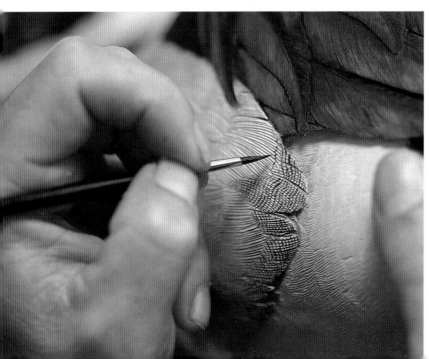

The vermiculation is painted at an angle perpendicular to the feather flow. Larry uses a sable Langnickel number 700 brush to paint the vermiculation. The color is a mix of Jo Sonya raw umber and black.

"It's important when vermiculating to keep the value of your paint consistent," says Larry. "Don't have some marks lighter or darker than others." Notice in this photo the feather splits Larry carved in this area.

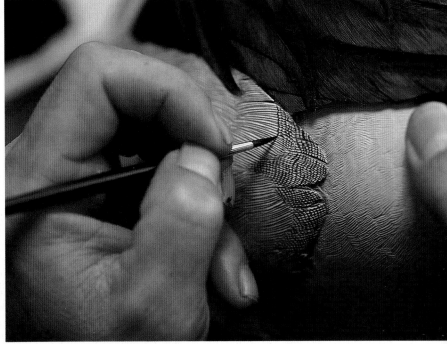

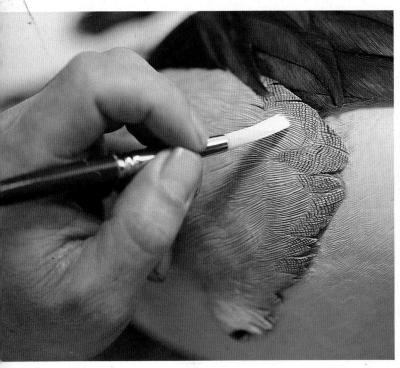

Before vermiculating further, Larry decides to lighten the area slightly by dry-brushing with white once again. Once the vermiculation process begins, you can alter the appearance of the feathers by adding more white by dry-brushing, or you can use a small brush to add white between the dark lines of vermiculation. Vermiculation, says Larry, is not especially difficult, but it is time consuming. It's important to refer often to reference material such as photos, study skins, and live birds.

This close-up shows the pattern of vermiculation Larry is using. The dark lines produce a herringbone effect.

A close-up of the finished vermiculation. *Photo by Tom Johnson.*

Larry's completed pintail pair. *Photo by Tom Johnson.*

2

Bob Swain
Hot Painting a Classic Shorebird

Duck hunting might be a shadow of what it once was, but more carvers than ever before are making hunting decoys, or decoys in the hunting tradition. Most of these contemporary wooden birds will never float in front of anyone's duck blind. They are tokens, symbols that represent finer times of wildfowl hunting.

Robert Swain, who lives on Virginia's Eastern Shore, doesn't hunt, but he makes shorebird and duck decoys that look like they might have come from Teddy Roosevelt's hunting rig. His carvings are eagerly purchased by hunters, who have no intention of taking them into the field.

Bob makes decoys the old-fashioned way, with a saw, a rasp, and a couple of knives. Then, before painting them, he performs the aging ritual. The bird is anointed with a pungent liquid (dirty paint thinner, says Bob) and set ablaze.

When the fire subsides—it's a controlled burn—the cedar has lost its fresh-cut gloss and looks as though it has been floating in a swamp for the past hundred years. At this point, Bob is ready to paint.

The painting process involves both pigment and fire: the paint is applied, diluted with thinner, then ignited. When the fire is out, the area is cleaned with a bristle brush, and the process is repeated until Bob arrives at the desired color and patina.

In making these instantly aged decoys, Bob is not trying to dupe buyers into thinking they're purchasing something from the 1890s. (He carves his initials into each decoy, and the month and year the bird was carved are stamped onto the lead bottom weight.) It's just that Bob, and those who buy his work, enjoy the fantasy that the bird was carved many years ago. They like the muted colors, the patina, the primitive shape.

In the past ten years or so, the market for wooden decoys has risen in indirect proportion to the decline in waterfowl populations. The irony is that although there are fewer birds to hunt than ever before, more hunting-style decoys are being made. The reason, I suspect, is that the decoy is the hunter's tangible link to a time we like to think of as more fruitful, more pure, a time when our planet could still support great populations of waterfowl. In an imperfect world, it is our means of revisiting a more uncomplicated era, our ticket to a time that has passed us by.

For this book, Bob Swain paints a preening dowitcher. He uses Ronan oil-base paints, which he says work well with the burning technique. These Ronan paints are intended primarily for sign painting and other graphic arts work. Their advantage in this application is purity of color, flat finish, and quick drying time.

As the session begins, Bob has already prepared the bird by applying dirty paint thinner and burning it off. This step ages the wood and darkens the surface. When the dowitcher is finished, some bare wood will show through, so it's important to make the wood appear aged.

Needless to say, you must be extremely careful if you try this technique yourself. Keep flammables away from your work area, and burn only a small area at a time. Burn outdoors in a safe place.

Bob describes this painting technique as constant experimentation. "I use the bird as a palette, mixing a lot of earth-tone colors until I get the value I want. Then the paint is burned."

The Ronan paints are very thick, and Bob dilutes them with mineral spirits, applying them in a series of washes. As paint builds up, it is buffed with a scrub brush before another coat is applied.

Burning oxidizes the mineral spirits and helps the pigment soak into the wood, resulting in a distressed, antiqued appearance. "I don't use any exact method or design in painting," says Bob. "It's more an attempt to provide an impression of a bird, rather than a literal description."

Although Bob is painting a dowitcher in this session, these techniques can be used for painting any waterfowl or shorebird species where traditional techniques and an aged patina are desired.

Bob has prepared the wood by burning off a coat of dirty paint thinner (the stuff he uses to clean his brushes), and he now applies a coat of white Ronan brand Japan paint to the head, leaving the eye and bill unpainted. The paint is thinned with mineral spirits.

The paint is ignited with a wooden kitchen match and quickly burns off.

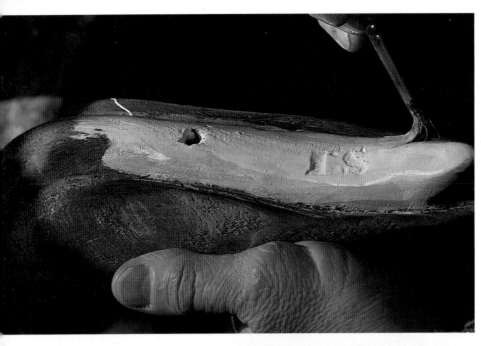

The same white
paint is applied
to the belly of
the dowitcher.

And again the paint
is burned, leaving the
surface blistered.

Bob applies a
second coat to the
head.

And this coat also
is burned. He will
repeat the paint/
burn cycle until
he gets the aged
patina he wants.

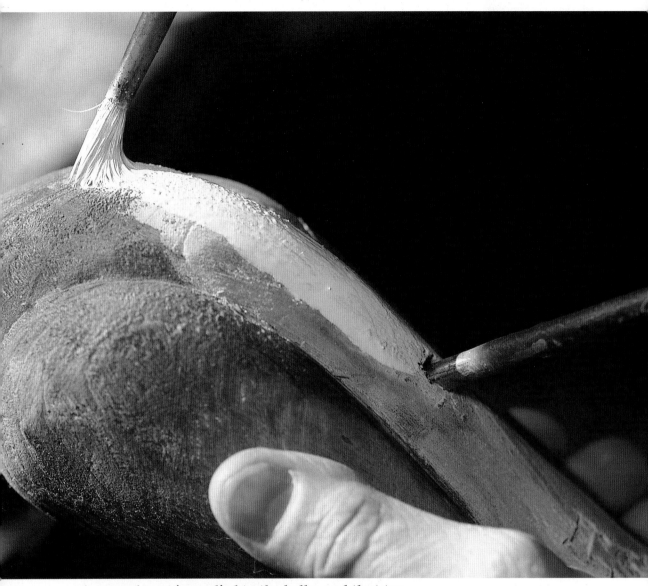

A second coat is applied to the belly, and that too is burned off. With each burning of paint, pigments are absorbed into the wood fibers and eventually build up on the surface. The burn lasts only a few seconds, but long enough for the heat to oxidize the paint thinner, leaving the scorched, blistered pigment. After several repeated applications, the built-up pigment will be removed with a brush.

The back is painted white, and the paint is burned off. Just after burning, the paint will look cracked, blistered, and generally unappealing. Don't despair. Blistered paint and built-up residues will later be removed, leaving only the paint that has been absorbed into the wood fibers.

Bob applies Ronan raw sienna to the neck, extending it into the white of the head.

The raw sienna is burned off; as it burns, the edges of the painted area become less distinct, appearing to blend with the surrounding paint.

The effect is heightened by buffing the painted and burned areas with a stiff brush. Brushing removes built-up paint residue and further blurs the margins where colors meet, producing a blended edge. It also polishes the surface of the bird slightly, enhancing the rapidly aging patina.

A coat of raw sienna mixed with a little raw umber is applied to the neck.

This color is blended into the breast area of the bird.

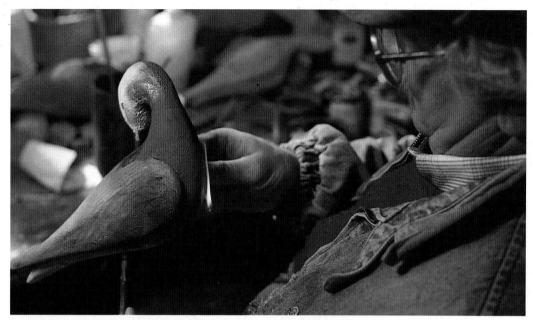

Then the paint is burned. The process of painting and burning is an inexact science, and Bob experiments often while he works, trying different colors or different combinations of colors. Burning, in this application, is part of the blending process. The process of burning and buffing makes the colors more muted, their edges less distinct.

Burnt sienna, Van Dyke brown, raw sienna, and a small amount of white are applied to the wing areas of the bird. "I don't mix the paints before putting them on," Bob says. "I use the bird as a palette and mix them on the wood." This coat also is burned.

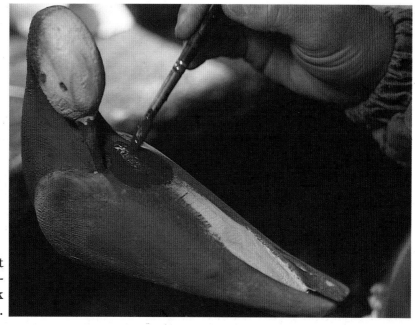

A coat of burnt sienna is applied to the back and wings.

The paint again is burned off. The paint-burn-buff process produces birds that are unique. Because the procedure is inexact, no two birds are alike.

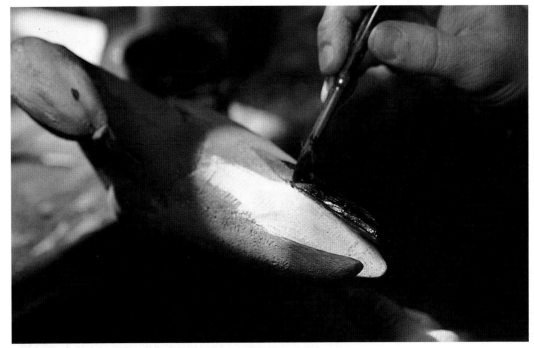

Bob now paints the wing tips with Van Dyke brown darkened with a small amount of black.

The Van Dyke brown is carried up the wing and blended into the lighter shade of brown along the sides of the bird.

This paint is then
burned off.

Bob uses a small brush to apply black paint to the eyes and bill.

The bill and eyes are burned with the kitchen match. Because these areas are small, they will not burn much. Often, Bob simply holds the match to the area long enough for it to blister the paint. Paint burns better when it is diluted with fresh thinner; thinner that has been sitting in an open container for a while loses some of its combustibility.

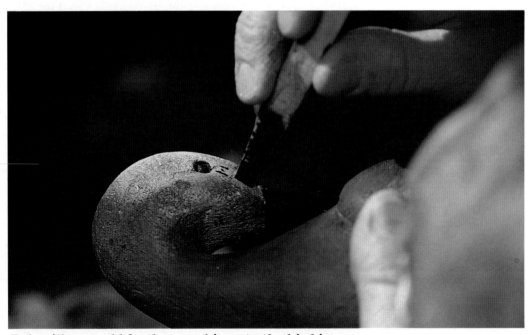

Bob will now add feather markings to the bird in a traditional method known as stick painting. A thin piece of wood approximately one-fourth inch wide is dipped in black paint and is used to dab feather markings along the head.

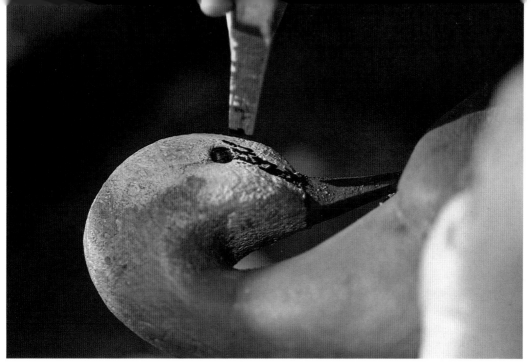

Bob begins in front of the eye and applies the black marks close together to create a shadow along the eye channel. The paint is applied directly from the can, so it is thick, and the marks are heavy. They will be reduced somewhat during burning and buffing.

The marks extend along the head and onto the neck.

Next, Bob applies feather markings to the top of the head. The area immediately above the eyes is left white, while the top of the head and the eye channels are darkened.

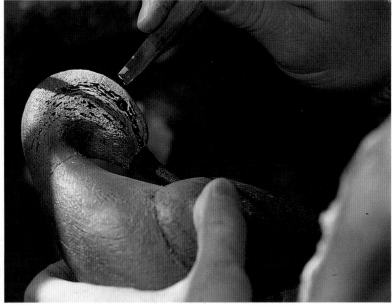

Now the markings are applied to the lower portion of the cheeks . . .

. . . and along the neck . . .

. . . and the breast.

31

Before burning the paint, Bob touches up a few of the feather markings around the eyes.

And then the black paint is burned. The feather edges are small, so they won't burn a great deal. Bob uses two matches here to singe the paint. A small propane torch or similar heat source would also work.

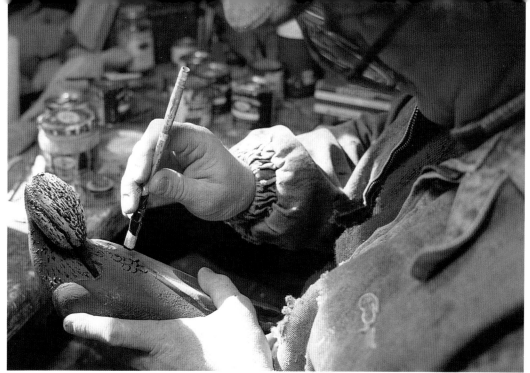

Bob begins applying the second series of feather marks using a similar technique. Old-time decoy makers often whittled a stick so its point produced a U-shaped feather mark. Bob accomplishes the same thing by wrapping a piece of sandpaper around an old paintbrush, dipping it in paint, and dabbing on the feather marks.

These larger markings are used for the wings and back of the dowitcher.

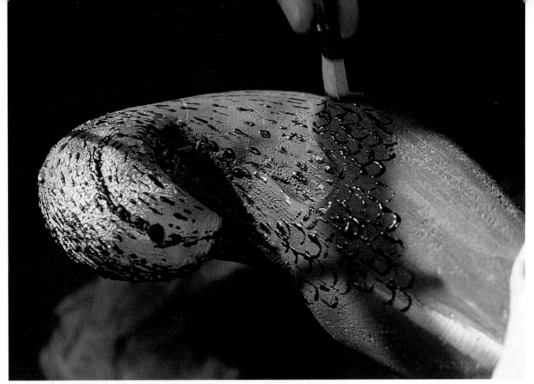

The feathers should be applied so that they run together, creating a layered flow. Practice on a piece of scrap wood before painting your bird.

These feather markings are burned.

Bob's next step in the aging process is to wash the dowitcher with soapy water and a stiff sponge or pot scrubber. The amount of pigment removed in this step is proportional to the amount of enthusiasm you use in scrubbing. Scrub until you achieve a patina that is pleasing to you.

The finishing touch is one final baptism by fire. Dirty paint thinner is applied to one area at a time and is burned. Use extreme care when doing this and don't burn the carving in an area where there are other flammables. Keep a fire extinguisher handy.

The completed dowitcher looks like this. The final
washing, burning, and buffing mutes the black
feather edges and softens the edges of the paint.
You can vary the amount of buffing to remove
more or less paint, or you can completely buff the
paint off in selected areas, producing the illusion
that the bird has been handled a great deal over
the years. The process is extremely variable, so
use your imagination. No two birds will be exactly
alike.

3

Rich Smoker
Painting a Scaup Head and Bill

Rich Smoker grew up in Selinsgrove, Pennsylvania, and developed an interest in waterfowl while hunting ducks in local ponds and along the Susquehanna River. A need for hunting decoys led him and his father to carve a rig of black ducks, mallards, and canvasbacks while Rich was in high school. His goal at that time was not a career in carving, but in the related field of taxidermy.

After high school, Rich entered an apprenticeship in taxidermy, and in 1979 opened his own business. Ironically, he began carving birds just as he was launching his taxidermy business, spending his slack season working with the carving tools.

"Other than that hunting rig, I made my first decoys for a contest in 1979, and began my first decorative a year later," he says. "I realized I could carve decoys, but not the way I wanted to, so I kept working at it. I knew the anatomy of the birds through taxidermy. I knew what they looked like from the inside out, but it was hard for me to take a piece of wood and make them look right from the outside in. I had no art education or background. I learned about mixing paints and using an airbrush in taxidermy training. When I finally discovered that carving had a lot in common with taxidermy as far as the sculptural aspects are concerned, I realized that carving wasn't as hard as I thought, and I began doing more of it and started to sell some."

Rich and his family moved to Crisfield, Maryland, in 1983 and he began to spend more time carving and less time doing taxidermy. In 1985 he quit taxidermy completely, except for preparing his own study skins.

Since the career move in 1979, Rich has won more than 230 ribbons in such competitions as the Ward World Championship in Ocean City, Maryland, the Mid-Atlantic in Virginia Beach, Virginia, the Havre de Grace and Chestertown shows in Maryland, the spring and fall shows in Chincoteague, Virginia, and numerous others. His decorative carvings and gunning decoys are in collections around the country.

In this session, Rich will paint the head and bill of a lesser scaup drake. To the uninitiated, painting the scaup head might seem fairly simple. In most field guides the head appears to be a consistent blue-black, without complicated design or color problems. You just mix the proper color and put it on. Right?

Not exactly. The head of the lesser scaup, when the sun hits it just right, can reflect a spectrum of subtle colors, lending the blue-black shade a depth and interest that is difficult to capture with paint. As the following photographs indicate, Rich begins painting the head not with blue and black, but with a psychedelic palette of colors. These colors, as the painting process continues, will become fairly subdued, but their presence will serve as a foundation for the darker colors, providing depth and dimension.

As the session begins, Rich has painted the body of the bird, inserted the eyes, and applied washes of black and white gesso to the head to produce a base coat of gray.

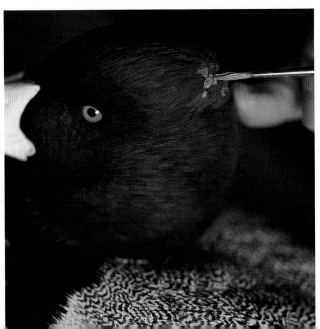

Because the head of the lesser scaup is deep blue, Rich uses a combination of mars black and white gesso as the final wash for the base coat. Mars black is a cold, bluish black and provides a good foundation for the colors to come later.

When Rich textured the head, he carved a fluffy area on the back of the head. Here he applies a base coat of warm white, raw umber, and carbon black to those feathers. This lightens them slightly to make each individual feather show up better.

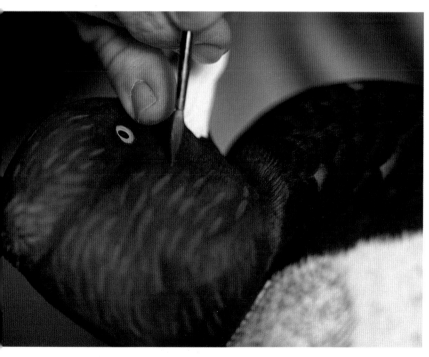

He uses the same base color to add subtle feather markings to the head of the scaup.

Rich begins mixing the colors he will apply to the head. "I use a lot of Jo Sonya paints on the body, but when I want an iridescent color on the head I switch to Liquitex, Hyplar, or Winsor & Newton because they don't have the gouache in them and are shinier," he says. "I also add pearl essence to the paint to give it gloss. I don't use metal flake because it tends to oxidize over time. Pearl comes from the ground-up shells of mollusks, so it should hold its luster forever."

Rich begins by laying out Liquitex permanent green deep, phthalo blue, violet, and dioxazine purple. He will combine these colors with pearl essence in green, lilac, shimmering blue, purple, and red to get varying shades.

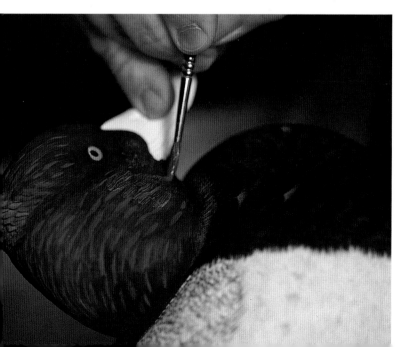

He blends the colors on the head of the bird, not on the palette. First he applies a little deep green, then adds some phthalo blue.

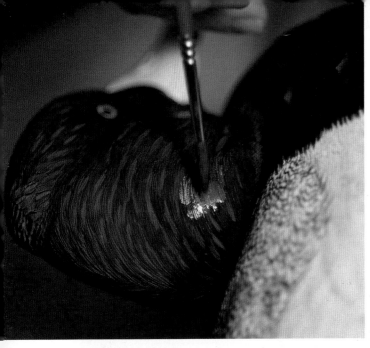

Green, blue, and purple are blended on the cheek of the bird. Pearl essence is added to the paint as it is applied.

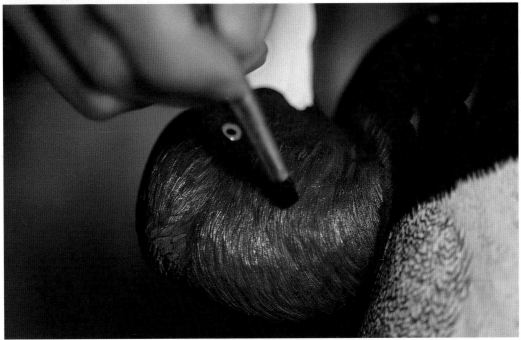

With a larger area painted, Rich switches to a Pat Godin-designed short-bristled brush to blend the colors together. The short, tapered bristles of the Godin brush are designed for efficient blending. Other brushes of similar size and shape would suffice.

The colors are not mixed totally, but are blended in sort of a colorful soup. "You keep layering the colors and changing the values," explains Rich. "You want to see some green, some purple, and some blue. As the blue and purple run together, they'll create a deeper value of violet."

Now he repeats the procedure on the left side of the head. The bright colors serve as a base. They will be darkened considerably with washes later in the painting process.

The top of the head is darker than the cheeks and gets a combination of blue and purple paints. "You want to show some iridescence on the top of the head, but it has to be subtle."

"You see more blue on the back of the crown, so I put some blue there and fade it into violet. Where blue and violet meet, I apply the violet first because it is a darker value."

Red produces a highlight when a little is mixed with the blue and purple.

Rich has added more green to the left side of the head. "Green is used as a low-point highlight," he says. "I follow that with blue and red, which will feed into the violet."

The Godin blending brush is used on the top of the head to blend darker values of blue and purple. The greens and reds are used primarily on the cheeks and the brow line.

The technique is a constant process of applying and blending paint until Rich gets the effect he wants. Basically, the top of the head should be purple, with violet and blue blended in. The cheeks have more red and green, which add depth and highlights. Rich uses pearl essence sparingly on top of the head, but more liberally on the cheeks and brow line. Obviously, some experimentation is called for.

With the base colors dry, Rich begins the wash on the back of the head. The color is black mixed with raw umber, diluted greatly with water. "The first wash has to be thin, or you might lift some of the pearl," says Rich.

The wash darkens the head, toning down some of the warmer values of the colors applied earlier. Washes should be applied very thinly. Apply as many washes as needed to subdue the warmer tones.

Rich uses a hair dryer to dry the paint between washes. Acrylics normally dry quickly, but the hair dryer speeds up the process even more.

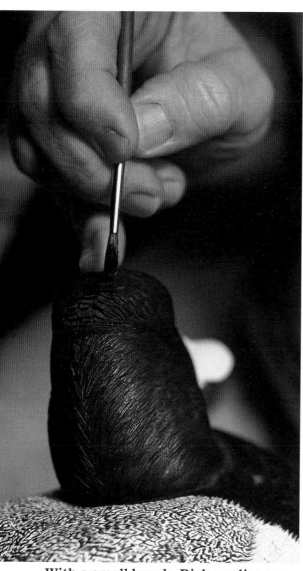

Another wash coat is applied over the area to tone down the iridescence slightly. This wash is made by combining Liquitex mars black (a blue-black) and Jo Sonya carbon black. The colors are diluted a great deal with water.

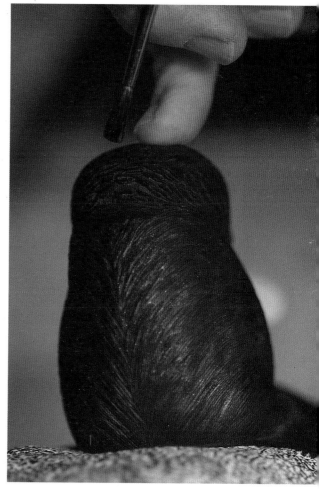

With a small brush, Rich applies some straight carbon black to the edges of the carved feathers on the crown of the head. The black provides the impression of a shadow, increasing the effect of having the feathers fluffed out.

"You have to be thinking about the painting when you're carving," says Rich. "The head is very dark on this species, and you have to make your own lights and shadows." A thin wash of carbon black settles into the textured area of the head, deepening the shadows and increasing definition. The bright colors applied to the cheek of the scaup do just the opposite. Because acrylics are transparent, the bright base color shows very subtly through the dark wash, creating highlights.

50

The small brush is used to apply black feather markings along the head.

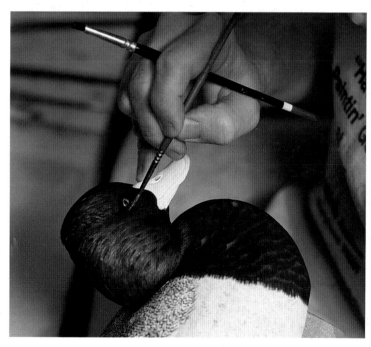

The mars black and carbon black combination is used to create shadows along the cheek and under the eye. Rich uses two brushes in one hand. The smaller brush is used to apply the paint, and the larger brush blends the colors.

The dark wash has toned down the values of the cheek and head, but still the colors provide iridescence and depth. Now Rich is ready to paint the bill, which he primed earlier with gesso.

For the bill he uses Liquitex and Grumbacher colors because they have a slight gloss. "I don't like to use too much blue on the bill," he says. "It should have just a hint of color."

The base color consists of phthalo blue, Paynes gray, and white. Rich adds just a slight amount of blue and gray to the white, then mixes in some white satin pearl essence. "A bill should have a lot of depth to it; the way to create this effect is to either apply a lot of washes of paint or use some pearl essence powder, which brings up the luster. The luster should show through all the coats of paint put on the bill."

Rich brushes on four coats of the white mixture; now he will add highlights and shaded areas with the airbrush. To prevent paint from spilling over onto the head, he covers the area with masking tape.

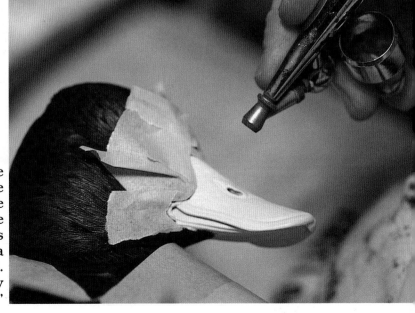

A little manganese blue is added to the base bill color, and he applies this with the airbrush. "This is nothing more than a blush," he cautions. "The colors are very subtle."

The blue is slightly darker closer to the head and lighter toward the tip of the bill. A little dioxazine purple is added to the original base color to provide a highlight. "This is just to show that there's something other than blue on this bill," says Rich. Care must be taken to keep this application very subtle.

Rich learned to use the airbrush as a taxidermist. Its advantage in painting the bill is that the airbrush can create very subtle tonal values. He begins spraying the lightest value of manganese blue, then adds slightly more color until he gets the tone he wants.

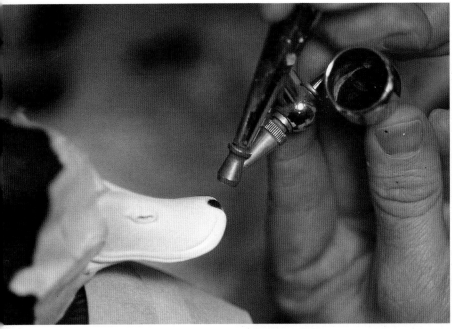

When the blue has been applied, Rich lightens the tip of the bill with white, then loads the brush with mars black and paints the nail. Mars black, with its blue cast, will provide the correct value on the blue bill.

Black is applied to the bottom of the bill with a small brush.

The inside of the nostrils are painted black.

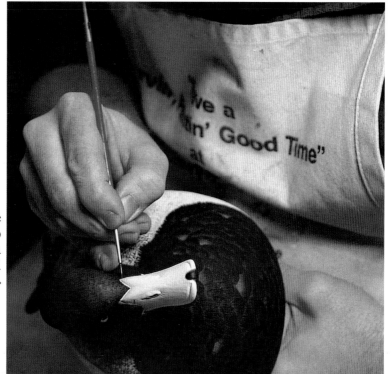

Rich finishes the job by touching up the transition area where the bill meets the head.

The completed pair of lesser scaup.

4

Rich Smoker
Painting a Brant Gunning Decoy

Although Rich Smoker has won many ribbons for his decorative carvings, gunning decoys are his first love, and one of his favorite hunting experiences is going down to Chincoteague Bay, putting out a string of brant decoys, and listening to the haunting whistle of brant as they come to the decoys in the dawn light.

The Atlantic brant decoy Rich is making here serves two purposes. It is intended as a practical, useful hunting decoy, and it also is symbolic of the tradition of brant hunting along the eastern seaboard where Rich lives.

The brant body is made of cork, one of the finest materials available for making working decoys because it is light in weight and floats in a very lifelike manner. Rich carved the body, carved and attached the head, and then sealed the cork with Bondo, the synthetic material used for repairing dings in automobile bodywork. (Assuming this bird is a drake, we'll name him James Bondo.)

"I figure that if Bondo is strong enough to withstand the abuse it gets on a car body, it should serve well on a decoy," says Rich. "Body filler is easy to sand, and it gives me a good smooth surface to paint."

After the Bondo is applied, the bird is sanded, a keel is doweled into the body for strength, and four to six coats of thick gesso are applied. After a light sanding, a finish coat of white gesso is put on, and James Bondo is ready for his paint job.

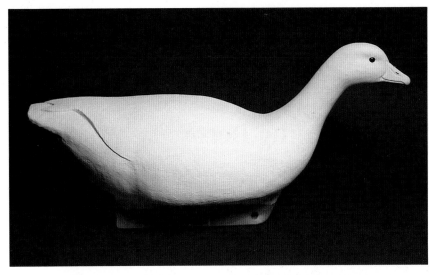

The cork-bodied brant has been sealed with auto body filler, sanded, and laden with four to six coats of white gesso. Rich applies as many coats as necessary to seal the bird and acquire a uniform surface.

He begins painting by applying base coats to the head, sides, back, and breast. The breast and head are painted with black gesso. The sides are white gesso tinted with raw umber, and the back is a mixture of white, burnt umber, and black gesso. The back is outlined with straight black.

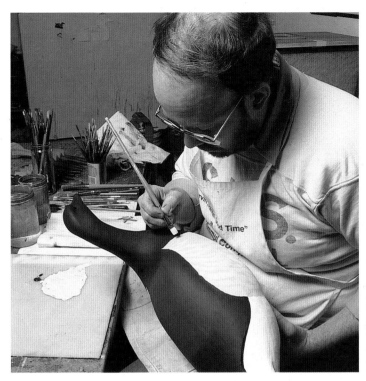

Once the base coats dry, Rich begins painting the sidepocket feathers. He uses white paint to which a little raw umber has been added.

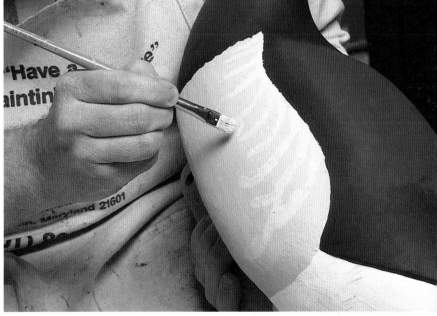

"Since this is a gunning decoy, you have to keep the paint fairly simple," he says, "but I want the sidepockets to really *look* like the sidepockets on a brant. I'm starting out with the white and raw umber and just delineating each feather, using a number 5 oxhair brush beginning on the left side."

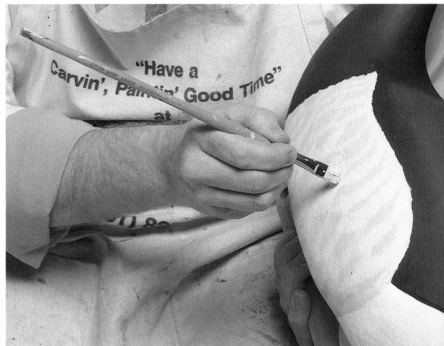

The brush Rich is using has very stiff bristles, and the paint is applied in almost a dry-brush technique. You want just enough paint on the brush to delineate the feathers, he explains.

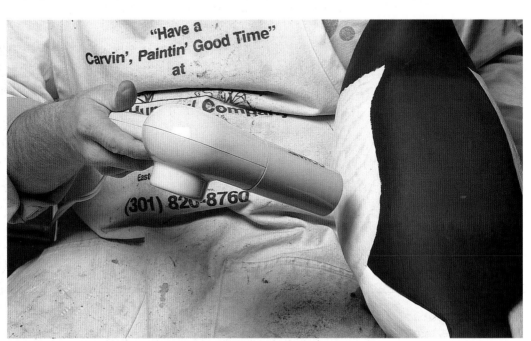

He uses the hair dryer to speed up the drying time.

With the feathers delineated in white, Rich will now paint the inside of each with raw umber, which he will mix in three different values. Raw umber mixed with white constitutes the lightest value. Straight raw umber is the middle value. And raw umber mixed with black is the darkest value.

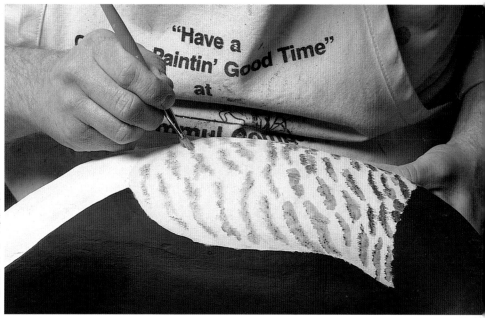

The darkest value is applied at the front of the sidepockets, and as Rich moves backward he uses the lighter values.

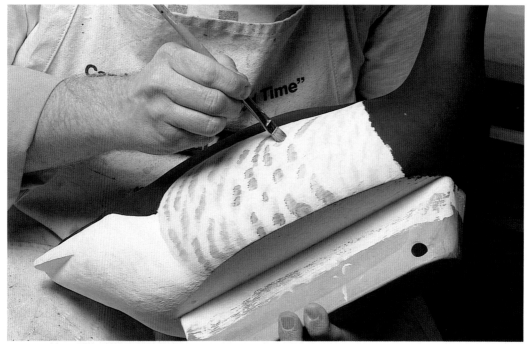

The same procedure is done on the right side-pocket of the brant, with the darkest feather edges applied toward the breast of the bird.

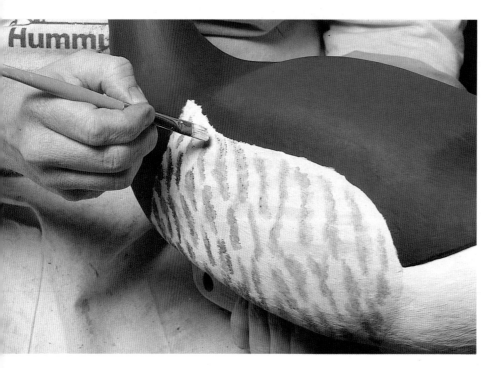

Rich returns to the left sidepocket, touching up the feather groups with a mix of white tinted with raw umber.

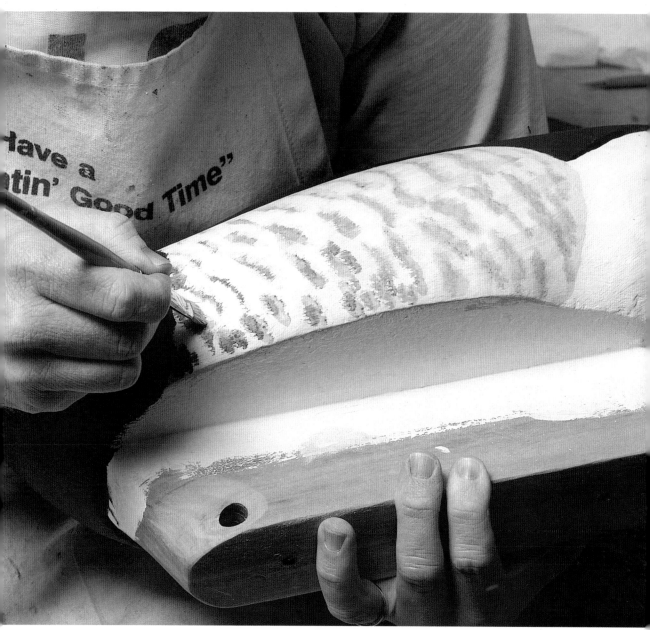

Next he applies the white/raw umber mix to the margins of the darker feather edges, making the sidepockets appear lighter from a distance. This step lightens the overall value of the sidepockets; it is done on both sides, making them approximately equal in value.

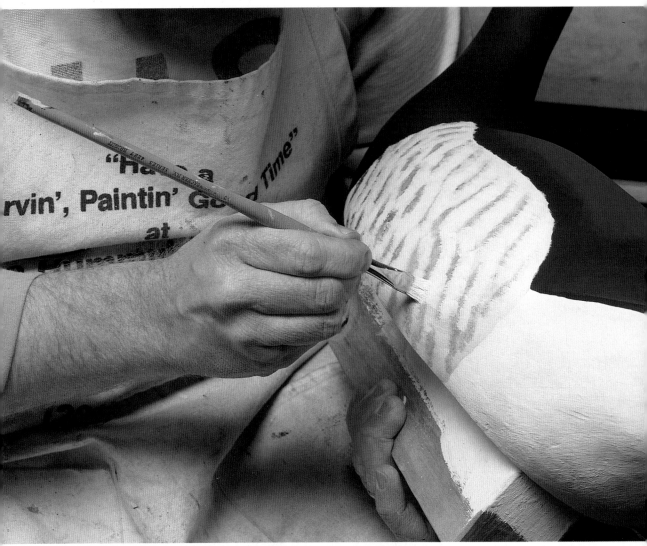

"I don't have any set pattern for painting the side-pockets," says Rich. "I make it up as I go along and try to enjoy each one. Often the sidepockets seem too dark after adding the raw umber feather edges. Then I go back with the white mix and reduce the size of the raw umber markings. Because you're working with a transparent medium, this technique helps produce an illusion of depth and softness, like you're seeing dark feathers just below thin lighter ones. It's a matter of experimentation and adjustment."

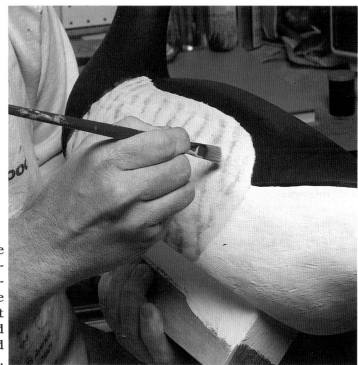

Rich again darkens the feathers on the left side-pocket before applying a light wash. "The idea is to alternate light and dark, light and dark, creating a layered effect," he says.

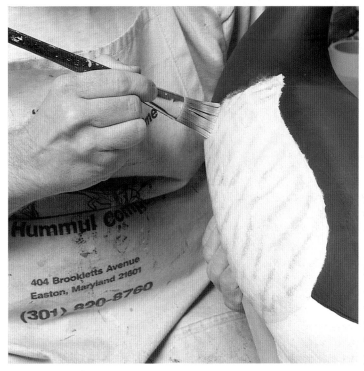

Another thin wash of white is used to tone down the area, bringing the values closer together. Rich uses a wide brush for this, applying the wash quickly. The washes should be very thin. Apply two or more to lighten the side-pockets further.

White tinted with raw umber is used with a small brush to paint horizontal lines along both side-pockets. "These marks give the feathers some movement, some flow," Rich says.

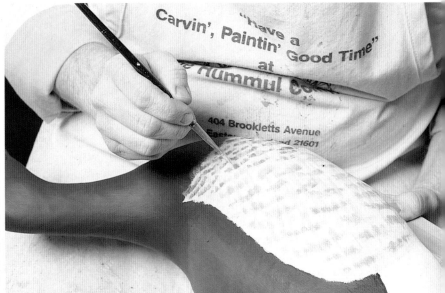

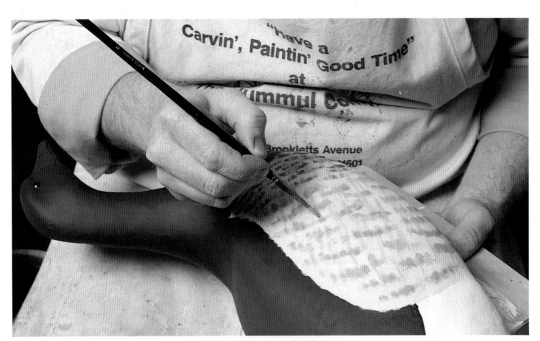

"Painting the sidepockets is sort of an evolutionary process," says Rich. "You apply dark over light, then light over dark, and let the color values build depth." Here he applies raw umber feather markings on the right side.

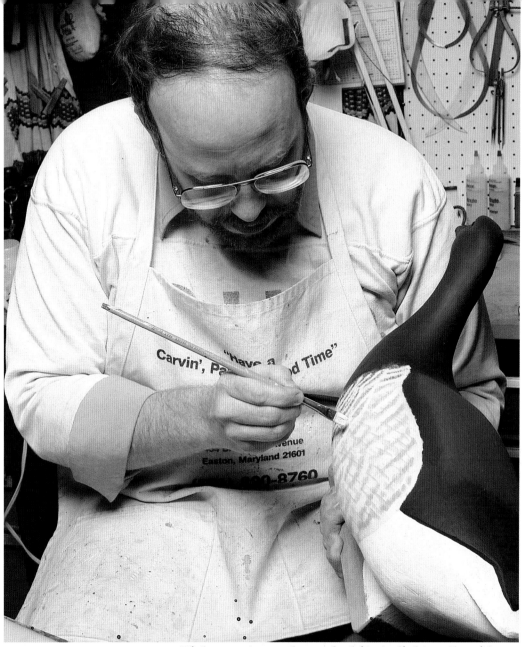

Rich uses two values of white to lighten the side-pockets. White gesso is tinted with Jo Sonya warm white, then with titanium white, which has a cooler, bluer value. These slightly different values of white are used in conjunction on the sidepockets. The values differ enough to help provide the illusion of depth and softness. Overlaying paint and combining warm and cool whites produces an almost limitless range of values, not simply stark black and white.

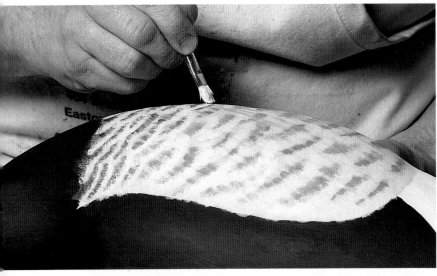

He lightens the feathers slightly at the rear of the sidepockets, but keeps the darker values toward the front. Rich alternately applies white and the darker values of raw umber until he is satisfied with the look of the sidepockets.

Although Rich is not painting individual feathers on this gunning bird, he refers to photographs to help him capture the overall look of the brant.

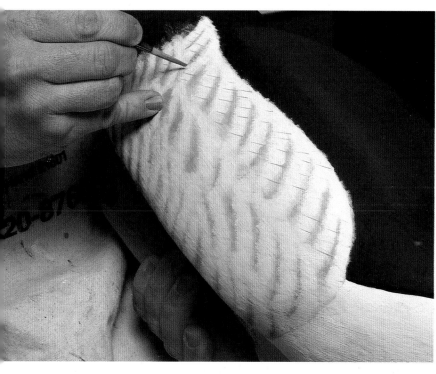

Satisfied now with the look of the sidepockets, Rich uses the small brush to apply some raw umber feather splits.

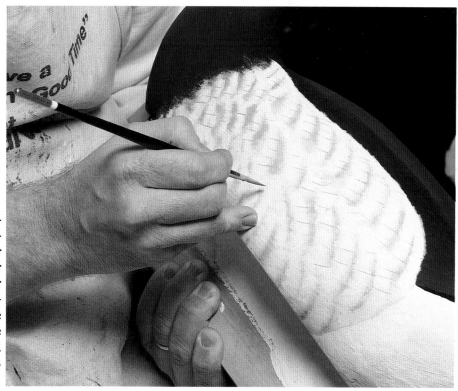

The three values of raw umber are used for the feather splits. Darker splits are applied at the front of the sidepockets and at the margins of the area.

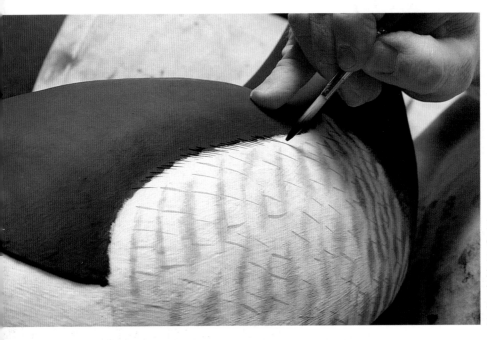

Rich uses the darkest value of raw umber to feather the area where the sidepocket meets the back.

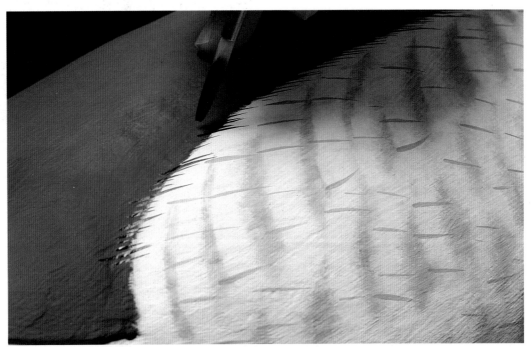

These marks, with the feather splits, provide a flowing design along the side of the bird.

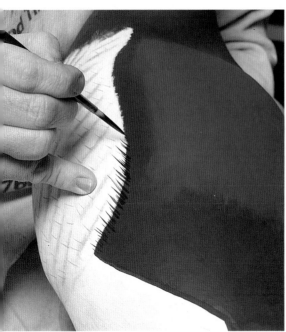

Similar marks are applied to the left side of the brant.

Areas that are too dark can be lightened by applying white over the raw umber.

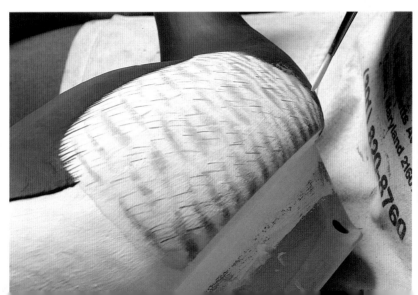

Rich's final touch is to add some white near the breast area.

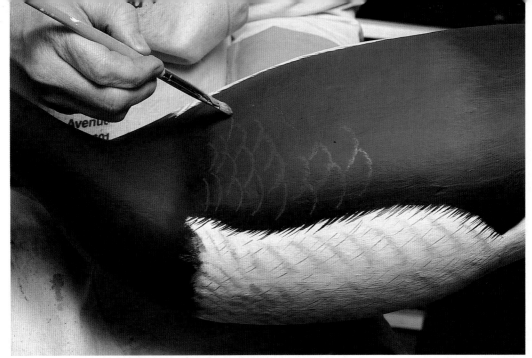

With the sidepockets completely dry, Rich now
paints feather markings on the back. The color is a
mix of white and burnt umber.

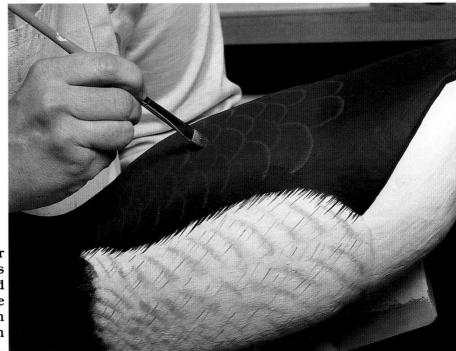

The feather
markings
are applied
with the same
number 5 brush
he used on
the sidepockets.

A lighter value of white and burnt umber is used to highlight the feathers. Rich applies just a touch of color to the back edge of each feather.

"On a gunning decoy, you don't want to see a lot of fancy feathers," says Rich. This technique produces a subtle effect that is traditional and pleasing to look at.

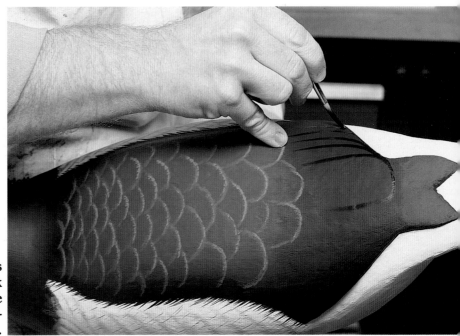

Rich uses straight black to paint the feathers overlaying the back.

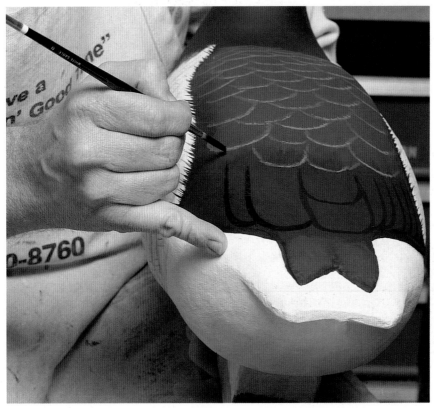

The effect is subtle, but these feather groups show up nicely against the base color mix of black, white, and burnt umber.

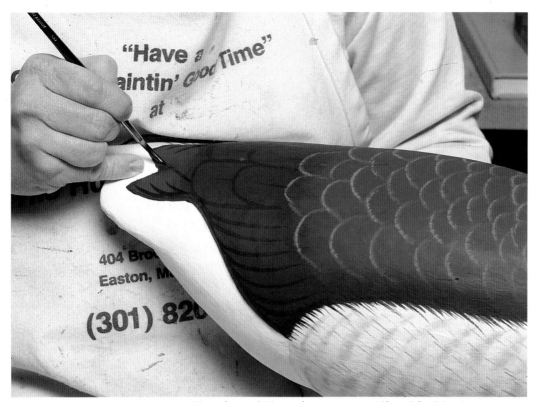

The tips of the wings are outlined in black.

Black is also used to outline the edges of the tail.

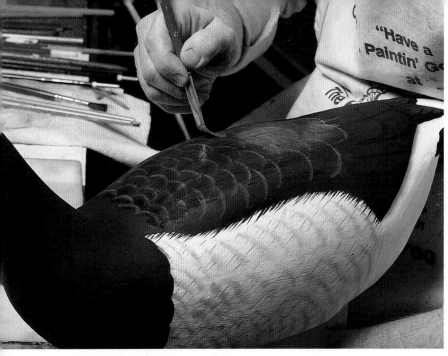

A thin wash of burnt umber and black is applied to the back of the brant.

This wash is also applied to the wings and the tail feathers.

78

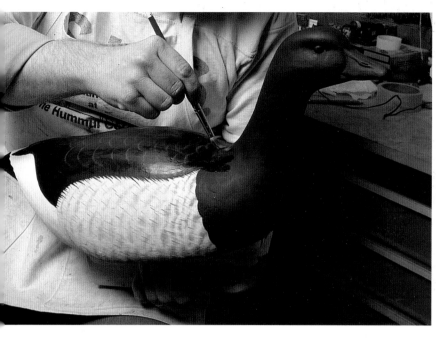

The burnt umber and black wash is diluted a great deal with water. Its purpose is simply to tone down the area, pulling the subtle values of feather detail closer together.

Rich is still not satisfied with the look of the side-pocket feathers, so before he paints the necklace and bill of the brant, he decides to darken this area by applying raw umber.

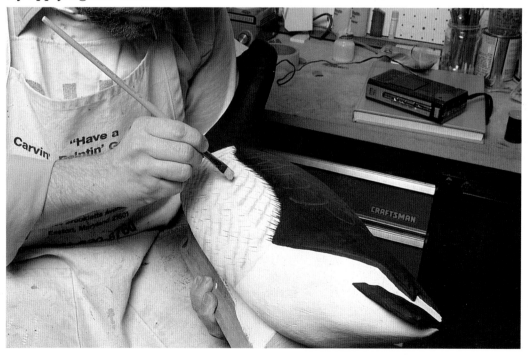

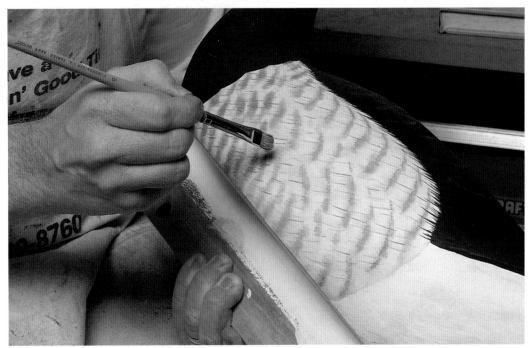

"When you go directly from a base coat to your lightest area, you have a tendency to make it too light," says Rich. "I want to make the center of the sidepockets a little darker, so I'm going to darken the edges a little."

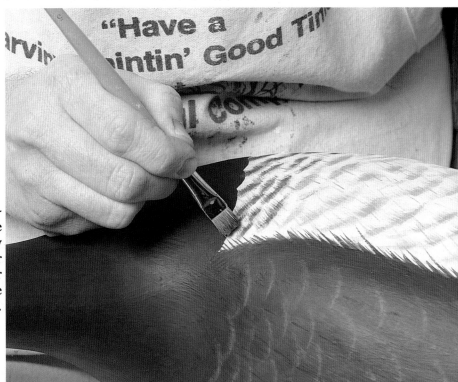

The darker side-pockets, he believes, now blend better with the feather detail on the back of the bird.

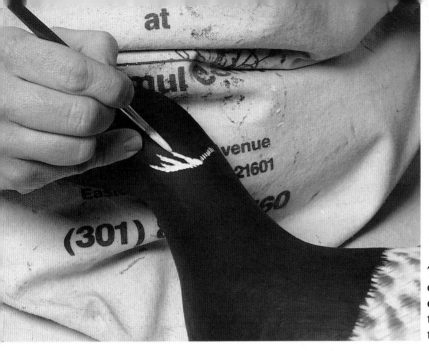

The white necklace of the brant is created by applying titanium white with the edge of a brush.

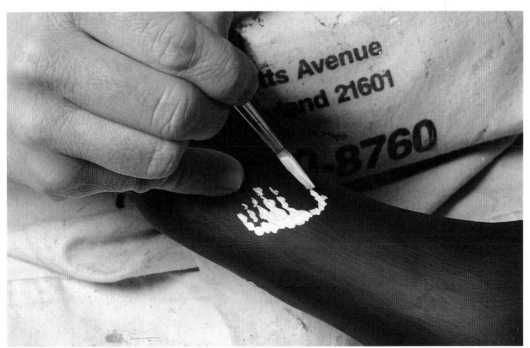

"Necklaces will vary from brant to brant," Rich says. He used a mounted study bird as a guide in painting this one. "You want some areas to be pure white and others to be light gray. That way you have the illusion of overlapping feathers."

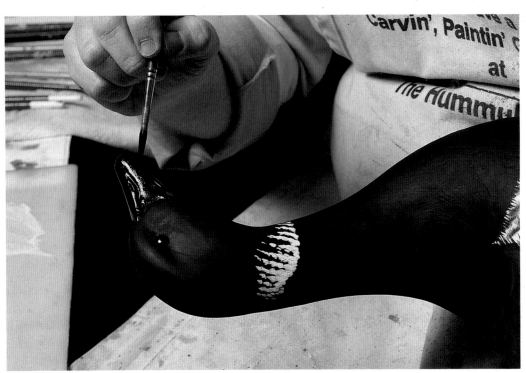

The bill is painted with Liquitex mars black. "That will give me a bit of a shine and create a demarcation where the bill meets the head," says Rich. "I'll also go over the tertials with the mars black."

The completed brant gunning decoy.

About the Author

Curtis Badger has written widely about wildfowl art, wildfowl hunting, and conservation issues in general. His articles have appeared in many national and regional magazines, and he serves as editor of *Wildfowl Art Journal*, which is published by the Ward Foundation. He is the co-author of *Painting Waterfowl with J. D. Sprankle* and is currently working on a book about salt marsh ecology.

Other Books of Interest to Bird Carvers

Songbird Carving with Ernest Muehlmatt
Muehlmatt shares his expertise on painting, washes, feather flicking, and burning, plus insights on composition, design, proportion, and balance.

Waterfowl Carving with J. D. Sprankle
A fully illustrated reference to carving and painting 25 decorative ducks.

Carving Miniature Wildfowl with Robert Guge
Scale drawings, step-by-step photographs and painting keys demonstrate the techniques that make Guge's miniatures the best in the world.

Decorative Decoy Designs
Bruce Burk's two volumes (*Dabbling and Whistling Ducks* and *Diving Ducks*) are complete guides to decoy painting by a renowned master of the art. Both feature life-size color patterns, reference photographs, alternate position patterns, and detailed paint-mixing instructions for male and female of twelve duck species.

Bird Carving Basics: Eyes
Volume one in the series presents a variety of techniques on how to insert glass eyes, carve and paint wooden eyes, burn, carve with and without fillers, and suggest detail. Featured carvers include Jim Sprankle, Leo Osborne, Pete Peterson, and Grayson Chesser.

Bird Carving Basics: Feet
Volume two features the same spectacular photography and detailed step-by-step format. Techniques for making feet out of wood, metal, and epoxy, creating texture and tone, and shaping feet in various positions are demonstrated by Dan Brown, Jo Craemer, and Larry Tawes, Jr.

Bird Carving Basics: Heads
Volume three illustrates how to create realistic head feathers by various methods, such as burning, wrinkling, stoning, and carving flow lines. Experts like Jim Sprankle, Mark McNair, and Martin Gates share their innovative techniques.

Bird Carving Basics: Bills and Beaks
Techniques such as burning and wrinkling, inserting a bill, using epoxy membranes, making open and closed bills and beaks, and carving the tongue are demonstrated.

Bird Carving Basics: Texturing
Volume five explores various ways of creating realistic looking feather detail. Includes over 200 close-up, step-by-step photos.

For ordering information and a complete list of carving titles, write:
Stackpole Books
P.O. Box 1831
Harrisburg, PA 17105
or call 1-800-READ-NOW